Getting Started

Just like a recipe, selling your home is a step by step process. This guide will offer suggestions in order to help a seller find a buyer, and move forward to a contract of sale.

To begin, the seller will simply use their *eyes* 👀 for the first step…

- Go out to the curb and look back at your home. Is it well manicured?
- Is the lawn mowed regularly?
- Are the trash cans hidden from sight?
- How does the paint look? Are the colors of the house neutral?
- Are there cracks in the driveway that need to be patched?
- Are there too many cars parked in front of the home?
- Do flower pots clutter the entrance?

Curb appeal is the very first step in the seller's recipe. Without it, you may as well not bother adding the other ingredients. The "lived in" look is not conducive to having nice curb appeal. As you face your home, it is not advised to talk yourself out of things that need to be addressed. If you look and see pink trim, don't tell yourself, "Well, my yard looks great, the pink won't matter." It will matter to every single buyer who pulls up. To the buyer, everything out front of the home is a sign of *coming attractions*. As a Broker, it was rare that I found a home unsavory at the curb, yet highly desirable inside. There were many times I had appointments set for showings, and would pull up with buyers in my car, only to have them say, "Forget it, let's go to the next house" due to the appearance of the front yard. No kidding, this happens. <u>Do not underestimate the power of the presentation</u>.

Spruce up the Exterior!

Assuming you have accepted that no homeowner is immune to the necessity of curb appeal, let's move to the next ingredient in our recipe, staging. Again, look 👀 from the front door, and simply stand there. In fact, face the exit of your home for a minute, and turn around quickly. Observe the first things that jump to your eyes. If the first glance is suddenly *not* the wonderful space in the room, the fantastic layout, and the warmth of the environment; we have a problem. If your eye immediately focuses on a colorfully faux painted wall, or the creative collage of family photos, the buyer will see those items and not much else.

They certainly won't be able to immediately see themselves in the space, because there is no blank canvas where that buyer can visualize their own belongings. Most people cannot truly see passed visual distractions.

I spent years and years taking over listings that just would not sell. I rarely needed to adjust the price, but ALWAYS needed to adjust the environment in a stagnant listing. Sometimes this process meant I had to take the home off the market for a week just to make the adjustments. Maybe it needed painting, or moving items around (or out), and once, I even completely repainted kitchen/bathroom cabinets just because they dated the home so intensely. My point is, spending a little time and money, in order to have a home "market ready" is worth every minute and dollar. Seller's may think, "Well, if I'm spending money on staging, then I should get more for my property." It is logical point, however, the goal of this staging investment is to have multiple buyers interested in your home. All interested because it looks great, the price is right, and they can see themselves in the space you have created for them.

If you are prepared to do the following, you are ready to move to the next ingredient in the recipe. Again, use your eyes and make a list…

- Is your entry free of clutter? No shoes? Backpacks? Mismatched rugs? Is it bright and/or lit up? (Having all of the lights **ON** is essential when showing a home)
- Do the walls only have one or two items hanging on them? No calendars, photos, or, the forbidden….posters?
- As I walk forward, does the couch create a wall that breaks up the space? Is there an entertainment center that takes up half the room? Do my items look like they are from the 1980's?

Okay, we need to have a side discussion regarding outdated furniture. Please note this is not to hurt feelings, it is simply one of the main ingredients in our recipe. I cannot tell you how many times I have heard how expensive a table, couch, or lamp was when purchased in 1997. This is completely understood. But go into your closet and look at your extremely expensive prom dress or tuxedo from the same year, and ask yourself, "Would I wear this outfit from 1997 today?" If the answer is "no", then please understand that decorating a home is the EXACT same thing. Furnishings from even 5 years ago are really consider "outdated".

That's not to say you have to repurchase new things every 5 years, but do realize the black lacquer end table is not going to appeal to someone trying to envision themselves in the space with today's stylings. It would be like me trying to convince my daughter to wear my prom dress to her prom today! I know, I know, "Well, the buyer can always change it". Unfortunately, that is just not how it works. Just like that prom date, they only have one chance to make a good first impression. Showing up in chiffon and puffed sleeves is just an immediate turn off. Don't do it!

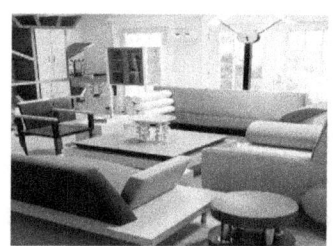

Back to the list…

- Are your countertops clear and clean?
- Are ALL of the windows open and clean for all showings?
- Do the overall colors of the home seem neutral and calm?
- Is there plenty of room for buyers to stroll?
- Are the baseboards dust free?
- Are electronics and cords hidden from view?
- Is the tub scrubbed, tile clean, toilet closed? Basically, has the maid done a deep cleaning?

It sounds like a lot, I know. Again, it's understood that you need to "live" in your home, but remember the goal. Within 60 days or less, you will not be living there anyway, so you may as well start boxing up those figurines and books now. Start the motion and momentum while at the same time, de-clutter!

Finally, ask a friend or extended family member (someone who will be honest with their opinion) to come by and give their first impressions of your new environment. LISTEN to the comments, and don't offer reasons why they are wrong. Rather, consider they may actually be offering some great feedback and critique. Another great thing to do is find some new housing tracts with model homes available. Take a tour and see how professional stagers have set up the models in the perfect way. Those homes are specifically created to sell the buyers on the feeling, emotion, and serenity they invoke. Take the time to go view, take notes, and even pictures of model home interiors, and use what you learn on your project.

Pricing

This is the *big debate*. Sellers make the mistake of trying to price high, because they can "always come down" in price. This will make your house sit on the market and have a stagnant appearance to buyers. They will wonder why it has not sold, and possibly think the house may have "issues". Remember, you are saving a ton of money selling yourself, so use some of that savings to undercut your competition.

If you are really struggling for a starting price do the following:

- Go onto Zillow and filter your search to "just sold" and compare those homes to your own.
- Ask an Escrow company to give you a list of everything that has sold in your neighborhood.
- Order a formal appraisal. These usually come in a little low, so pad it a bit.
- Go on a tour of other homes in your area to compare the features of your competition.

Please keep in mind "listing price" IS NOT the same as "selling price". Do not look at another home currently for sale and assume that is the current value of the property. It is not. Your comps should be based on homes similar to your own which have SOLD. A property must be exceptional, and pristine in order to go above the sold comps. Choose your list price with that awareness and education.

Marketing Prep

The next step in the house selling recipe is preparing to go to market. Now that you have your home shiny and perfect, it is time for photographs. Pictures are the most important part of marketing your home. People do not usually take this step very seriously because they figure, get the basics done, and the buyer will see the house when they visit. If you do not use professional, clear, wonderful photos online you will lose at least 1/3 of potential buyer eyes. With so much imagery on social media, people only spend time on photos that draw them in and keep them looking. Make your home stand out.

Sellers (AND AGENTS) often make the mistake of looking through the lens of a camera and picking out a specific object with their eye. Much like taking a picture of a person standing in front of them. **Pull back**. Get the whole room. Get an image of the entire space, from wall to wall, not the couch or bed sitting inside of the room. You'd be surprised how much this mistake happens. In addition, when photographing the exterior, make sure to take the photo from roof eve tip to roof eve tip, no cut-offs. Look on line and see what appeals to you, then try for yourself. If photography is just no your thing, consider hiring a professional. They range between $200-$400, and worth every penny. Professionals have those cool wide angle lenses and tripods which enable them to get the WHOLE picture. Take many, many images, and go through them to select the 20 best.

Now that you have the photos of your newly staged, cleaned, and updated home, get ready to create your marketing materials. You will need to write a large paragraph describing your home. List the bedrooms, bathrooms, unique features, square footage of the home/land, proximity to schools and town, age of home, even available showing times. Don't forget contact information!

For years I have stuck with one real estate listing website to do just about everything for me. It's simple and very user friendly. **Listingproducer.com** not only allows you to purchase an individual web address and website for your home, but you can create flyers as well. It practically does the whole thing for you, so don't be intimidated by the idea of creating a website. It's not what you think. You upload your photos, chat about your house, and the program does the rest. They have great customer service, and you own your web address for 1 year for just about $32.00. Once you have the web address locked down, you can then add it to your signs, your other ads, and your flyers. You need that web address, for sure, absolutely! Most agents use the address itself, like, "123MeadowStreet.com"; however, I suggest trying to lock down, "MeadowStreet.com" without the numbers if you can. Buyers might not remember the street numbers, but they may remember the street name when searching for your property on line.

Time to order your signs. Our office sells posts and signs, however, if you decide to buy your own, there are many online sources. You should without-a-doubt order a "rider", which is a long, thinner sign that hangs under your main "For Sale" sign, or sometimes above it. This should have any other message you wish to convey. Perhaps, "swimming pool" or "½ acre"; things buyers may not be able to see from the street. Riders are where you should place your web address in big bold letters for drive-by potential buyers. I always use a company called, "**Build-a-Sign**". They have a very user friendly website, and excellent customer service with quick turnaround time. While you are ordering those riders, think about ordering open house signs/stands as well. You will need at least 3 for directional purposes.

Another idea is to attach a flyer box to your sign (Build-a-Sign has these). If you decide this, make sure to keep it filled. You will need to print flyers with photos, a brief summary about the property, and don't forget your contact information!

Every time I list a property, I immediately send between 500-1000 post cards out to all of the neighbors. This is a simple project. Give a call to any of the local escrow companies, and ask them to farm and create labels for 1000 homeowners surrounding your address. The Escrow company will hope you will keep them in mind when you sell, and they will be anxious to prove their good customer service to you. Pick up your labels, and stop by the post office for a long role of postcard stamps. **"Vista Print"** seems to have the post card system down. There is really no need to go elsewhere. DO NOT buy the oversized postcards thinking you will make a bigger impact. Oversized postcards cost as much as a letter, so don't go there. Sending out post cards to neighbors creates a buzz. Perhaps someone down the street will want tell a friend about the new home for sale in the neighborhood. Maybe the post card will land in a buyer's hands who wants to downsize or expand their living situation, but stay in the same neighborhood. Hit every marketing front, don't miss a step.

After you have exhausted the typical marketing for a home, it's time to start your social media campaign. This should be the last step because it is such an instantaneous form of marketing, and all of your other marketing should already be in place prior to the media launch. Upload your "listing" to everything you can think of on social media. **Facebook, Instagram, Trulia, Linkedin**, and the best and biggest, **Zillow**. Zillow has a unique feature in the front of every listing. It allows you to walk your property and video the home. Sellers and agents never use this feature and I think that's a mistake. Go ahead and give the viewers a tour. Another great website is of course, **Craiglist**. Here is one important thing to remember with Craigslist; you need to do a "new posting" about once per week, rather then simply "refreshing" your posting. You want your posting to jump up to the top of searches, and the only way to accomplish that it to create a new posting. In addition, think about posting on a

Sunday, when folks have a day off to browse. You may even try posting in another category, like say, "furniture" just to get to those who may not be looking under Real Estate. The more eyes the better.

The First Phone Call/Email

The first phone call from your marketing efforts may very well be a real estate agent. Agents are trained to sell you on why they can sell your property. It's hard to say no to such compelling arguments, but keep your eye on the goal. The real estate agents will also ask if you are willing to "cooperate" with Brokers. This means that if they bring you a buyer, you will agree to pay them 2.5%-3% commission for that buyer. This defeats the purpose of your mission. If you were "cooperating" with agents, you may as well throw your house on the MLS and let everyone into the game. Your mission is to protect your bottom line, your net, the extra $20,000, $30,000, $50,000 you are trying to save by selling yourself. So get readying to say "No, thank you" A LOT.

With the first buyer call keep it simple. Don't try to sell anything. If there are questions, keep the answers extremely simple. Do not explain the entire history of the home, give them a reason to come and take a look for themselves. Set an appointment and prepare for the showing.

The Showing

Remember, lights on, window blinds open, toilet seats down! Prep the entire home. ALL ANIMALS PUT AWAY. There is nothing worse than the break in the rhythm of a showing by a barking dog. This is a serious matter. I am a huge dog lover, truly, but this must be said. There is a pace, a dance, a flow that becomes immediately halted by barking, meows, and even pet birds. It's hard to describe, but it's real. Do you know when a dog is focus intensely on a cat and the owner claps his hands to snap his attention away? Well buyers walk into your home and begin to focus with the same intensity. They picture themselves living in the space with all of their energy, almost a meditative trance. This breaks immediately with the distracting piercing sound of a bark or squawk.

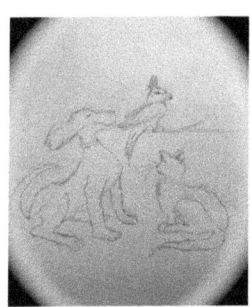

Pets + Showings = No Sale

Appeal to the senses of the buyer for the showing. Perhaps very soft music, forget the cookies baking, use strategic plug-ins instead. I like to have random plug-in air fresheners (maybe two) with the scents of the given seasons. Do not use powerful scents ever, but instead say, Gingerbread in December, and something tropical in the spring.

When the buyer comes to the door greet them and invite them into the showroom you have created. Now **STAND BACK**. This is where sellers make a huge mistake. I have had people tell me, "nobody knows my home better than me" and proceed to talk the buyer's ear off. It is too overwhelming to hear so many details on the first showing. Let the buyer feel the environment. Let them stroll and picture themselves living there. Please, please don't tell them about the new carpet you just installed or the new counters, they can *see* what is there. Allow the buyer to just observe. If there are questions, they will ask. Keep the responses short, and do not elaborate. Strictly the facts. Do not make the mistake of trying the "sell" the home. If you have followed all of the ingredients in the recipe, the house will sell itself. This is a complete practice in self restraint.   Perhaps re-read this paragraph if needed as a reminder.

Seriously, I understand the impulse to oversell, but think of that guy at the car

lot...do you enjoy the long drawn out sales pitch or do you only want the

answer to the question you are asking about the vehicle?   Remember, don't

be the car salesman when selling your house

The Open House

An open house is a great way to have your showings happen at the same time. It may even create a sense of urgency between buyers if they see other buyers looking and interested. You previously ordered 3 "Open House" signs; time to use them. You will need to place a "line ad" under open houses. A large ad isn't really necessary, but that is a personal choice. It is however, necessary to create a Craigslist ad announcing the open house with photos and the times. Place your open house signs starting at the closest main street with the arrow pointed in your direction. Continue with the next sign, and again, there should be an open house sign directly in front of your home with the arrow pointed to the property.

Have all doors open, soft music, and always have snacks & water bottles. Stand back, but stay standing and alert, ready for questions. Agents usually do not enjoy open houses because it can be long, weekend-burning, and unproductive work. Try to keep in mind, it only takes one buyer to see the open house, walk through, and decide to submit an offer.

The Paperwork

Everyone knows the phrase, "disclose, disclose, disclose". While going through the process of preparing your home, prepare your disclosures so they will be ready when your first offer comes in. List everything, both negative and positive about your home. This will be given to the buyer after the offer and acceptance is in place. During this *disclosure prep* you should call a reputable termite company to come and do a formal inspection. This cost ranges from $60-$100 usually. It is not necessary to have a *home inspection* as the buyer will have their own inspection through the process. Pest inspections may be called out by lenders, and it's good to have the knowledge of those repairs ahead of time, and disclosed up front in order to prevent further price reductions later in the process through negotiations.

One last idea so we have a beginning, middle, and close! Be sure to hire an experienced Lawyer or Broker who will get you through the contracts. An attorney will be a minimal fee (perhaps just a couple of hours) to review your docs. Most Brokers will check out your file for a couple hundred dollars. Today there are even virtual TCs – "Transaction Coordinators". They will complete the entire paperwork process for a very low fee. There is a great deal of liability attached to these documents, so make sure that all of your hard work is rewarded with a successful escrow and closing!

www.ingramcontent.com/pod-product-compliance
Lightning Source LLC
Chambersburg PA
CBHW051207170526
45158CB00005B/1856

9 781083 152428